# T.E. Lawrence and Clouds Hill

Wareham, Dorset

THE NATIONAL TRUST

*Above* Lawrence with Leonard Woolley at Carcemish in 1913

*Right* 'Suddenly Feisal asked me if I would wear Arab clothes like his own while in the camp … I agreed at once, very gladly; for army uniform was abominable when camel-riding … and the Arab things, which I had learned to manage before the war, were cleaner and more decent in the desert'. Photographed by Harry Chase in 1919

*Far right* A British Handley Page biplane being welcomed by the Arab forces at Um el Surab in 1918; painted by Stuart Reid (Imperial War Museum)

# HOW 'LAWRENCE OF ARABIA' CAME TO BOVINGTON CAMP

THOMAS EDWARD LAWRENCE was born on 18 August 1888 at Tremadoc in Wales. His father, Thomas Chapman, had abandoned an unhappy marriage and estates in Ireland to live in obscurity with the woman he loved. This was Sarah Junner, formerly his daughters' governess.

In 1896, after moving home several times, 'Mr and Mrs Lawrence' finally settled in Oxford. There, living off a modest investment income, they brought up and educated their five sons. They were never free to marry, but their relationship remained a secret.

Lawrence gained First Class Honours in modern history at Oxford in 1910. By then he had already visited the Middle East, researching a thesis on the architecture of Crusader castles. In 1911 his passion for archaeology and travel took him to the British Museum's excavations of the Hittite city of Carchemish in northern Syria. He continued to work there until the First World War.

Early in 1915 Lawrence was posted to the British Military Intelligence office in Cairo. He soon became an expert on the Arab provinces of the Turkish Empire, and sought to promote schemes for a rebellion. At last, in the summer of 1916, the Emir of Mecca took up arms against the Turks, starting the Arab Revolt. Soon afterwards Lawrence went to the Hejaz on an Intelligence mission to discover what was really happening and suggest ways to provide effective support.

The quality of his reports and his success dealing with Arab leaders soon led to a long-term liaison posting. Thereafter, he played a key role in the campaigns that led to the capture of Damascus in October 1918.

He then returned to England, personally committed to a long-drawn-out political campaign for Arab self-determination. In his own eyes, one of his greatest achievements was the political settlement reached at the Cairo Conference in 1922. Working as adviser to Winston Churchill, then Secretary of State for the Colonies, he had successfully argued for self-government in both Iraq and Jordan.

In the summer of 1922 he completed the 'Oxford Text' of *Seven Pillars of Wisdom*, an account of his experiences during the Arab campaigns. By then, however, the accumulated stress of his wartime privations, three years of political campaigning, and work on the book had taken a heavy toll. Sensing that he was on the verge of mental breakdown, he looked for a safe haven.

He remembered how, during the desert war, he had envied the uncomplicated lives of the British armoured-car crews. The ranks seemed to offer a place of safety, where he could escape for a time from all responsibility.

Lawrence enlisted in the ranks of the RAF using the name 'J. H. Ross'. After only a few weeks, however, the *Daily Express* revealed that 'Lawrence of Arabia' was serving at Farnborough as 352087 A/c Ross. In January 1923 he was dismissed from the Air Force as too great an embarrassment.

Close friends quietly arranged for him to re-enlist, this time in the Tank Corps. He arrived at Bovington Camp on 12 March 1923, as 7875698 Pte T.E. Shaw.

## LAWRENCE RENTS CLOUDS HILL

*'I covet the idea of being sometimes by myself near a fire.'* T.E. LAWRENCE, 4 OCTOBER 1923

*Above* The lintel to the front door is carved with the Greek words 'ου φροντις', which can be loosely translated 'Why worry?'

*Right* This view from the crest of Clouds Hill was painted for Lawrence by Gilbert Spencer in July 1925. Lawrence incorporated it into the panelling of the Music Room

*Far right* The cottage is set into the wooded slope of Clouds Hill

As Lawrence had hoped, routine life in the Tank Corps made few demands on his intellectual energy. In his leisure time he was free to pursue his strongest personal ambition, which was to write. Soon after arriving in Bovington he asked Jonathan Cape, the publisher, to send him some translation work.

Meanwhile, friends were urging him to issue *Seven Pillars* in a private subscription edition. In the autumn of 1923 Lawrence agreed to produce about 100 lavishly illustrated copies, printed on hand-made paper. To keep the book to a single volume, he would reduce it to 250,000 words, 84,000 words less than the existing Oxford Text. He would also be responsible for every aspect of production.

Knowing how difficult it would be to work on *Seven Pillars* in an army camp, Lawrence rented Clouds Hill. He wrote to his mother: 'I've taken a little cottage (half ruinous) a mile from camp, and water-tighted it to act as a work-room for myself. There I hope in future to do my writing, which is becoming more and more a habit.'

Clouds Hill had been built in 1808 as a simple labourer's cottage. It was probably once the home of a forester on the Moreton Estate. But for its association with Lawrence, it would almost certainly have disappeared by now, like many similar buildings of its time.

When Lawrence first saw it, the cottage was dilapidated. It had been unoccupied for years except by passing tramps. To pay for essential repairs, he sold the gold dagger made for him in Mecca during the war. He removed a partition-wall on the first floor and installed a large window in the roof. That gave him a good-sized room with enough light to work on his fine-press edition of *Seven Pillars*.

Lawrence's views on decoration were strongly influenced by neo-medievalism and the ideas of William Morris. Years later, he would comment that Clouds Hill had no paint or plaster or wallpaper. It was decorated with 'panelling; bookshelves; bare wood and undyed leather.'

As time passed, he would re-create in the cottage the atmosphere of his two previous homes, the tiny bungalow built for him in his parents' garden at Oxford, and the archaeologists' house at Carchemish. Each had been a simple structure brought vibrantly to life by the intellectual quality of its contents. Clouds Hill might be little more than a shell with a single furnished room, but it was also a place for reading, writing and listening to music. By the time he died, its contents would be extraordinary.

# THE TANK CORPS YEARS, 1923–5

*'No bed in the cottage, but picnic fare if you warn me. Don't expect a palace: it's a private soldier's idea of one, and very unfinished at that.'* T.E. LAWRENCE, 21 FEBRUARY 1924

By mid-November 1923 both the upstairs rooms were in use, the larger as a workroom and the smaller as a pantry. Lawrence slept and ate his main meals in Bovington, so he was untroubled by the lack of a kitchen or bedroom.

At this period the larger downstairs room was damp and unused, while the 'bathroom' probably contained little more than a washstand. Water could be fetched in buckets from a nearby spring, but the flow was less than a gallon a minute.

The task of revising and abridging *Seven Pillars* proved far more difficult than Lawrence had expected. After setting it aside for eighteen months, he was unable to recapture his earlier frame of mind. He now felt remote from the text and intensely critical of its style.

His revisions took into account the comments of critics such as Edward Garnett, Bernard and Charlotte Shaw, and E.M. Forster. The last came to Clouds Hill more than once to help. The Shaws also visited, as did Thomas Hardy and his wife, and friends from the ranks. On these occasions the workroom doubled as a sitting room. Lawrence would offer his guests tea and tinned snacks.

As each section of *Seven Pillars* was completed, it went to Lawrence's printer in London. Therefore, while revising one section he had also to correct proofs of others. Progress was slow. He had planned to work each day after his Tank Corps duties, but was tired and easily distracted. He spent from 4.30 till 9 pm at Clouds Hill, nearly every day, but would often 'dream, or

write or read by the fire, or play Beethoven and Mozart to myself on the box. Sometimes one or two Tank-Corps-slaves arrive and listen with me ... but few of them care for abstract things.'

One letter to Charlotte Shaw describes the cottage on a stormy April day: 'Inside it is calm as ever. We went out in the drift and looked under the rhododendron for dry stakes: and have got enough to make a red fire, in whose heat the damp fir-logs burn away freely'. They passed the afternoon reading and listening to music, and ended, 'when the dark comes, with a movement out of a Bach thing for two violins. We always finish with that, if the time is dark enough.'

Lawrence greatly preferred the RAF to the Tank Corps. In August 1925, after repeated requests, the RAF took him back. He was stationed first at Cranwell and then in India. Clouds Hill was out of reach, yet he decided to buy it. For the next three years it was sometimes let, and sometimes loaned to friends or members of his family.

*Above* Lawrence at Bovington camp about 1924

*Left* William Roberts's *Camel March*; one of the illustrations commissioned by Lawrence for the lavish subscribers' edition of *Seven Pillars of Wisdom*

*Far left* The Music Room in 1935

*'I have lavished money these last three months upon the cottage, adding a water-supply, a bath, a boiler, bookshelves, a bathing pool (a tiny one, but splashable into): all the luxuries of the earth. Also I have thrown out of it the bed, the cooking range: and ignored the lack of drains. Give me the luxuries and I will do without the essentials.'* T.E. LAWRENCE, 21 DECEMBER 1933

On 13 May 1935, returning from Bovington on his Brough Superior motor-cycle, Lawrence was involved in a road accident. He died six days later without regaining consciousness. He was 46.

*Right* The maquette for Eric Kennington's tomb effigy of Lawrence in nearby Wareham church

*Far right above* Lawrence's abridgement of *Seven Pillars* was a bestseller

*Far right below* A model of the *Biscuit*, the speedboat used by Lawrence during the Schneider Trophy races in 1929 and later to explore the coastline of south Devon

Lawrence returned to England in January 1929. By then there had been an important change in his outlook. His *Seven Pillars* had won high praise, both as literature and as a printed book. Collectors keen to buy one had been offering over ten times the original subscription price of 30 guineas.

A popular abridgement, *Revolt in the Desert*, had been a bestseller, spurred on by rave reviews. Lawrence gave the royalties to charity, but was deeply proud of his hard-earned status as a writer. He had meanwhile completed a second book, *The Mint*, and started to translate Homer's *Odyssey* for the American book-designer Bruce Rogers.

At last, he seemed to be escaping from his 'Arabian' reputation. He wrote to Edward Garnett: 'In the distant future, if the distant future deigns to consider my insignificance, I shall be appraised rather as a man of letters than as a man of action.'

His twelve-year term of enlistment was to expire in 1935. After that, he planned to live at Clouds Hill. The advance for his *Odyssey* translation had paid off the purchase price, and the American trade edition sold astonishingly well. He spent almost all the royalties remodelling the cottage.

Among his first purchases was 'a moving forest of rhododendron', with flowers of differing colours to add variety to those already on the hillside. An outdoor 'convenience' was built, and a thatched garage for his motor-cycle. He had the main downstairs room damp-proofed and fitted with bookshelves. By the end of 1933 his book collection, previously stored by friends, was in place. There was also an ingenious water supply and a bathroom equipped with a water-heater and enamel bath.

The next project was a large water-tank, excavated in his neighbour's garden on the far side of the road. Its prime purpose was to protect the two cottages from the very real danger of heath fires, but he put a glazed building over it with space for a room at one end. He planned to install a printing press there and produce fine books.

By the end of 1934 most of the work had been completed, and the appearance of the cottage was much as it is today. Lawrence wrote to a friend: 'The little place is finished, so far as its main lines go, but a part of my leisure will clearly be spent in tinkering with details – as well as in the less satisfying jobs of keeping it clean, and cutting wood for my fire, and looking after the place generally.'

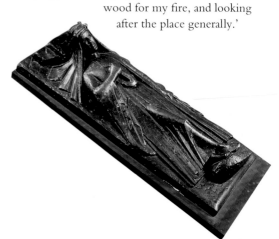

REVOLT IN THE DESERT

By

'T. E. LAWRENCE'

T. E. LAWRENCE *from a portrait by* AUGUSTUS JOHN

LONDON

JONATHAN CAPE 30 BEDFORD SQUARE

1927

'T.E. was an expert at "mixed grills" where men were concerned. He presided over the company, settling arguments, patiently answering all manner of questions, feeding the gramophone, making tea, stoking the fire and, by some magic of his own, managing without effort to keep everyone in good humour.'

ALEC DIXON REMEMBERS
VISITS TO CLOUDS HILL

*Right* The Music Room today

*Far right* This 1922 painting by Henry Scott Tuke may be a portrait of Lawrence

# TOUR OF THE HOUSE

*Take the stairs up to the first floor*

## The Music Room

Lawrence set up the main first-floor room at Clouds Hill in the winter of 1923–4, as a place where he could work, read and listen to music. For many, this room will always be associated with the writing he did here. His subscribers' abridgement of *Seven Pillars of Wisdom* has become a classic of 20th-century English literature.

### Furnishings

The furnishings are simple and practical. He commissioned local craftsmen to make the panelling and the fender. He bought a carpet and most of the furniture in London, though Mrs Thomas Hardy later added the coffin stool.

The landscape by Gilbert Spencer built into the panelling above the window is a view from the crest of Clouds Hill, painted while Spencer was staying at the cottage in July 1925. The only later changes seem to have been the rugs, probably received as gifts, the candleholders on the roof-beam and the candlesticks on the mantelpiece. These were a leaving-present from friends in the RAF Marine Craft section, when Lawrence's twelve years' enlistment ended in 1935.

### Listening to music

After shelves were put up in the downstairs room, he would have done most of his reading there; but he still used the upstairs room for listening to music, writing and entertaining visitors. Music was important to him. While living in London in the early twenties, he had gone to concerts frequently, usually on his own. This had helped him to cope with the stress of his political battles and the effort of writing and rewriting *Seven Pillars*.

From 1922 onwards he was usually out of reach of concert halls (though he continued to hear live performances whenever he could). Instead, he bought recorded music. His gramophones were among the finest of the time, and he looked after them with the enthusiasm of a hi-fi fanatic. To get the best results, he used only fibre needles, dusting his records with fine graphite powder to reduce surface noise. If a record became noticeably worn, he would replace it. The gramophone now in the cottage, his last, was made by E.M. Ginn of Soho Square, London.

Lawrence's preference was for orchestral and chamber music. His favourite composers were Beethoven, Bach and Mozart. But his listening went well beyond the mainstream classics. He subscribed to recordings of early music published by *L'Anthologie Sonore*, and at the same time explored the work of contemporary composers.

## The Bunk Room

In the early 1920s, when Lawrence was working on *Seven Pillars* in what is now the Music Room, this smaller room served as a pantry. At some point he added an iron bedstead for visitors, later replaced simply with a mattress on the floor.

In 1932 Lawrence had an ingenious water system installed to serve the bathroom immediately below. A small hydraulic ram fitted to the spring in the garden opposite drove water uphill, under the road, and into the large tank above the cottage staircase. The tank, which can be seen from this room, had to act as a reserve, because the water supply from the ram was barely more than a trickle. At times it dried up altogether.

It was not until his last weeks at Clouds Hill in 1935 that Lawrence redecorated this room. As there was hardly any storage space in the cottage, he made a bunk-bed with drawers underneath. To damp-proof the walls, he covered them with aluminium foil. Finally, only days before his fatal accident, he fitted a porthole for ventilation.

A friend had obtained this for him from the breakers of the 1914 battle cruiser HMS *Tiger*.

## The Staircase

The portrait of General Allenby on the staircase is a copy of a pastel by Eric Kennington, commissioned by Lawrence as an illustration for *Seven Pillars of Wisdom*. The original, bought for Lawrence by his friend Edward Garnett, hung here until 1935 but was given by Lawrence's executors to the National Portrait Gallery.

Lawrence also owned Augustus John's 1919 portrait of Emir Feisal, used as a frontispiece to the subscribers' *Seven Pillars*. He wrote to Garnett: 'I shall have my dual mastership preserved in my cottage for all my time. It will be a queer, rich feeling. In the flesh that double allegiance was difficult: but the two quiet heads on the wall will let me do what I please. I shall grow philosophical, at finding that problem solve itself.' After his death the Feisal portrait was given, as he had requested, to the Ashmolean Museum.

*Above* Eric Kennington's pastel portrait of General Allenby once hung over the stairs. The original (now in the National Portrait Gallery) has been replaced by a copy

*Right* The Bunk Room in 1935

*Far right* Lawrence's translation of Homer's *Odyssey* helped to pay for his alterations to Clouds Hill

## THE BATHROOM

Lawrence's liking for hot baths may have harked back to his parents' comfortable Victorian home in north Oxford. During his twelve years as a serviceman, his letters recount how, in successive camps, he had contrived to heat water for washing. He saw the water supply, water heater and bathroom at Clouds Hill as one of the most important benefits paid for by his *Odyssey* translation.

To obtain a suitable bath and heater he went to R.G. Goslett, who had been supply officer at Akaba during the Arab Revolt and in peacetime ran a plumbing-supply business in central London.

The unusual cork tiling gave the room a feeling of warmth.

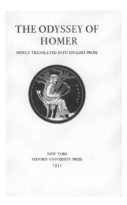

THE ODYSSEY OF
HOMER

NEWLY TRANSLATED INTO ENGLISH PROSE

NEW YORK
OXFORD UNIVERSITY PRESS
1932

Above Lawrence's reading
chair in the Book Room

Right The Book Room today

Far right The Book Room in
1935, when it was still filled
with Lawrence's superb library

## The Book Room

While Lawrence was at Bovington Camp, this room was damp and unused. After he left in 1925, it was fitted out as a kitchen so that friends and occasional tenants could live in the cottage.

Lawrence did not want a kitchen. At Clouds Hill he would eat prepared food from tins, or go to a café in Bovington. In the spring of 1933 he had the room damp-proofed and fitted with bookshelves. He then sent down several hundred books that he had previously stored with friends in London.

For reading during the day he made a 'proper lying-place' in front of the window, consisting of a large mattress covered with cowhide. For evenings and cold weather he designed the armchair and stainless-steel book-rest in front of the fire. He also designed the fender and the iron candleholders on the mantelpiece.

### Books

After Lawrence's death, his books, one of the most valuable assets in his estate, were listed and then sold by his executors. Looking at the room today, it is hard to imagine the extraordinary library that it once housed.

Lawrence had admired fine printing since his student years at Oxford, when he had first planned to run a private press of his own. In the early 1920s, while a Fellow of All Souls, he had assembled a remarkable fine-press collection. It included a magnificently bound Kelmscott *Chaucer*, a set of the five-volume Doves Press Bible, and books from the Ashendene Press and many other craft printers. These beautiful examples of fine printing were his most treasured possession. He wrote, 'I'd rather keep them than anything I've ever had'. They were shelved mainly in the narrow bookcases at each end of the room, where the leather and vellum bindings were protected from strong light.

The shelves on the side-walls contained English prose and poetry, including many works by contemporary writers. There were also books in Greek, Latin, and French – all of which Lawrence read. Inscribed copies by living authors testified to his friendships in the literary world. There were personal inscriptions from Edward Blunden, Winston Churchill, Joseph Conrad, C. Day Lewis, Charles Doughty, James Elroy Flecker, E.M. Forster, Edward and David Garnett, Robert Graves, James Hanley, Thomas Hardy, Llewelyn Powys, Siegfried Sassoon, Bernard Shaw, H.G. Wells and Henry Williamson. Ten books on these shelves were formally dedicated to him.

The shelving at Clouds Hill was designed to house more books than Lawrence then owned. One reason was that he had been unable to keep many of the books he had read during his years in the ranks. In the last months of his life he visited second-hand bookshops looking for the titles he lacked. Nevertheless, some shelves were still empty when he died.

## The Water Tank and Study

For a long time, Lawrence considered making more space at Clouds Hill by adding an extension. In 1933, however, he embarked on a different scheme.

The cottage was in danger throughout the summer from heath fires. As protection, he had a pool excavated in the garden across the road, fed by the spring and large enough to contain 7,000 gallons of water. When there was a fire, the local fire brigade could draw from it.

In 1933 Lawrence had the pool covered over with a glazed building. At one end there was a room, referred to as a study. In the last months of his life he was planning to install a printing press there and print, as his first book, a private edition of *The Mint*. The office had double doors on one side, inside which he mounted the two magnificent carved doors that he had brought back from Jeddah in 1921.

The pool is no longer watertight, but its outline can be seen from the first floor of the cottage. The glazed building that covered it has gone. Lawrence's Jeddah doors are now in the Ashmolean Museum.

All that survived of Lawrence's printing project were 100 collotype copies of the intended frontispiece, Augustus John's last sketch of him in RAF uniform, drawn in January 1935.

*Left* Lawrence covered the water tank with a glazed building (now gone). At the far end are the carved doors from Jeddah